Canticles of the Earth

Canticles
of the Earth

Celebrating the Presence of God in Nature

F. LYNNE BACHLEDA

LoyolaPress.

CHICAGO

LOYOLAPRESS.

3441 N. ASHLAND AVENUE
CHICAGO, ILLINOIS 60657
(800) 621-1008
WWW.LOYOLABOOKS.ORG

Cover design by Megan Duffy Rostan
Interior design by Megan Duffy Rostan and Erin VanWerden

Library of Congress Cataloging-in-Publication Data
Bachleda, F. Lynne.
Canticles of the Earth : celebrating the presence of God in nature /
F. Lynne Bachleda.
p. cm.
ISBN 0-8294-1732-X
1. Nature—Religious aspects—Christianity. I. Title.
BT695.5.B32 2004
242'.2—dc22

2004001768

Printed in the United States of America
04 05 06 07 08 Bang 10 9 8 7 6 5 4 3 2 1

To Ellen

It is possible to pray at all times, in all circumstances, and in every place, and easily to rise from frequent vocal prayer to prayer of the mind, and from that to the prayer of the heart, which opens the kingdom of God within us.

St. John Chrysostom

Acknowledgments

First and foremost, gratitude goes to Phyllis Tickle, a sage and funny woman and longtime friend and mentor who sent me to Joe Durepos. I have Joe to thank for bringing me into the Loyola family, a publishing house where something is deeply right. Joe also directed me to Brian Doyle, who sent me in rewarding directions in my search for Roman Catholic voices. Thanks especially for Chet Raymo.

The authors, some of whom are anonymous, and the anthologists are credited in the bibliography and in the rights and permissions section at the end of this book. It is obvious that they made this volume possible, and they gave me a renewed appreciation for words that stand the tests of time.

For life itself and the love of the land, I thank my parents, Fleeta and Al. May the substantial best of you live on in me.

Ellen Morefield has provided solid encouragement, more praise than was at times due, sound thinking to guide me through the rough spots, and concrete aid at deadline time. For her lifetimes of loving understanding, caring, and support, I am indeed grateful beyond words.

Finally, immeasurable thanks goes to my past, present, and future animal and human friends, especially Jane Braddock. You make the journey possible and a joy.

Introduction

Canticles of the Earth is a collection of writings gathered to help you see the natural world through a spiritual lens. It is a book for everyone. You don't have to go on exotic expeditions to have access to the countless riches of the natural world. By simply paying closer attention to the view out your window, a vase of flowers on your kitchen table, a cat in your lap, the dog at your side, or the song of birds in your nearby park, you can immerse yourself in nature's holy brilliance.

With the guidance this book provides, you can come closer to the consolation and contentment the Divine holds for us outside. You can behold your own spirit through the lens of the treasure-laden Earth and understand how profoundly and steadfastly we belong to this wonderfully blessed host.

Many selections in this volume derive from the Christian tradition, but you may also come to fresh perspectives on this spirit-filled world with the Buddhist, Jewish, Hindu, Muslim, Shinto, indigenous, and secular voices also here. This multiplicity of traditions points to the reassuring fact that in nature we are never alone, for humanity has always sought the sacred in creation.

This devotional handbook has 160 selections. It is arranged so that practitioners who keep the fixed hours of daily prayer can use it at "dawn," "day," "dusk," and "dark." If you keep this worshipful schedule, you can have forty days of natural contemplation. *Canticles of the Earth,* however, is also completely suited for reading several passages at one sitting, or contemplating only one random passage now and then.

St. Ignatius championed "seeing God in all things." He would surely agree that the outside world is God's own cathedral. In any season, in any locale, nature is an architecture for the Spirit, whose abiding foundations are splendor, diversity, power, and mystery, and whose soaring magnitude inspires us without limits.

You are welcome to come outside and worship. Come be at one with your nature.

EVERY DAY IS A GOD, each day is a god, and holiness holds forth in time. I worship each god, I praise each day splintered down, splintered down and wrapped in time like a husk, a husk of many colors spreading, at dawn fast over the mountains split.

I wake in a god. I wake in arms holding my quilt, holding me as best they can inside my quilt.

Someone is kissing me—already. I wake, I cry "Oh," I rise from the pillow. Why should I open my eyes?

I open my eyes. The god lifts from the water. His head fills the bay. He is Puget Sound, the Pacific; his breast rises from pastures; his fingers are firs; islands slide wet down his shoulders. Islands slip blue from his shoulders and glide over the water, the empty, lighted water like a stage.

Today's god rises, his long eyes flecked in clouds. He flings his arms, spreading colors; he arches, cupping sky in his belly; he vaults, vaulting and spread, holding all and spread on me like skin.

ANNIE DILLARD
from *Holy the Firm*

Day

BE IT IN THE WOODS, on the beach, in the desert, down by the swamps, in the mountains, or on your city apartment steps, the comfort that arises outside comes from being in the presence of cumulative intelligences of different species that are much older and wiser than we are. Conceivably, we are urged to learn from nature. It is possible that when Jesus advised us to "Consider the lilies of the field," he meant don't worry about earthly details, but he also literally meant what he said: "Consider the lilies."

There are voiceless insights to be gleaned from the species that surround us, if only we would stop to be with them. There are practices to profit from in God's manifest expression in a creek. There are practices to release God's unmanifest energy in the "all" it will take to become a blade of grass. Part and parcel of forming and fading away, there is a flawless balance between creation and destruction in nature. Here are the lessons that can help us lighten our own losses. Only if we take the time to become a quieter vessel can the always available grace of God course into us.

F. LYNNE BACHLEDA

Dusk

IN THE NAME OF GOD, stop a moment, close your work, look around you.

LEO TOLSTOY

 *Dark*

PEOPLE SAY THAT WALKING ON WATER is a miracle, but to me, walking peacefully on the earth is the real miracle.

Thich Nhat Hanh

PIED BEAUTY

Glory be to God for dappled things—
    For skies of couple-colour as a brinded cow;
        For rose-moles all in stipple upon trout that swim;
Fresh-firecoal chestnut-falls; finches' wings;
    Landscape plotted and pieced—fold, fallow, and
            plough;
        And all trades, their gear and tackle and trim.

All things counter, original, spare, strange;
    Whatever is fickle, freckled (who knows how?)
        With swift, slow; sweet, sour; adazzle, dim;
He fathers-forth whose beauty is past change:
            Praise him.

                                    GERARD MANLEY HOPKINS

Day

IT WAS A DEAD SWAN. Its body lay contorted on the beach like an abandoned lover. I looked at the bird for a long time. There was no blood on its feathers, no sight of gunshot. Most likely, a late migrant from the north slapped silly by a ravenous Great Salt Lake. The swan may have drowned.

I knelt beside the bird, took off my deerskin gloves, and began smoothing feathers. Its body was still limp— the swan had not been dead long. I lifted both wings out from under its belly and spread them on the sand. Untangling the long neck which was wrapped around itself was more difficult, but finally I was able to straighten it, resting the swan's chin flat against the shore.

The small dark eyes had sunk behind the yellow lores. It was a whistling swan. I looked for two black stones, found them, and placed them over the eyes like coins. They held. And, using my own saliva as my mother and grandmother had done to wash my face, I washed the swan's black bill and feet until they shone like patent leather.

I have no idea of the amount of time that passed in the preparation of the swan. What I remember most is lying next to its body and imagining the great white bird in flight.

I imagined the great heart that propelled the bird forward day after day, night after night. Imagined the deep breaths taken as it lifted from the arctic tundra, the camaraderie within the flock. Imagined the stars seen and recognized on clear autumn nights as they navigated south. I imagined their silhouettes passing in front of the full face of the harvest moon. And I imagined the shimmering Great Salt Lake calling the swans down like a mother, the suddenness of the storm, the anguish of its separation.

And I tried to listen to the stillness of its body.

At dusk, I left the swan like a crucifix on the sand. I did not look back.

TERRY TEMPEST WILLIAMS
from *Refuge: An Unnatural History of Family and Place*

 *Dusk*

TAKE TIME TO LISTEN to the birds,
the waves,
the wind.
Take time to breathe in the air,
the earth,
the ocean.
Take time to be still,
to be silent,
to allow God to fill you up
with deep peace and love.

MAIREAD CORRIGAN MAGUIRE
from *The Vision of Peace*

THE HOUSE WOULD NOT DO. I had to be outside! I can only imagine what the neighbors thought if they saw me on my knees in my quite nice, upper-middle-class, suburban backyard that summer night. (I was a renter.) As I collapsed face to the earth, sobbing, and then swung skyward, the only other place I knew to look, I was screaming to a powerful face of God, "What *is* it that you want from me? *What* is it?"

I was desperate, broken down, broken open, and broken up. My heart was broken, too—my body deserting me as it swung me wildly into a regular panic. I wanted to jump out of my skin. Worst of all, I couldn't make any of it stop: nothing worked not prayer, not will, not patience.

So I was on my knees holding on to the grasses, bending low to hang on for not-so-dear life. I expect I was silent, but now I am not so sure. I was alone and as lonely as I had ever been. Yet while I anchored myself to the ground in prayer and lifted my pleas to the skies, I forged an essential connection with all the ancient families of faith and the people whose prayers made them live, all the people who have lived on the earth.

F. LYNNE BACHLEDA

 *Dawn*

ALL OF MY LIFE has been a relearning to pray—a letting go of incantational magic, petition, and the vain repetition "Me, Lord, me," instead watching attentively for the light that burns at the center of every star, every cell, every living creature, every human heart.

CHET RAYMO
from *Natural Prayers*

AS OFTEN AS YOU CAN, take a trip
out to the fields to pray.
All the grasses will join you.
They will enter your prayers
and give you strength to sing praises to God.

RABBI NAHMAN OF BRATSLAV

 *Dusk*

IN RANDOM ARRAY on the warm dusky autumn
ground,
Your grace summons, sighs,
"Come, soul. Lay breath down. Rest. Dream."

F. Lynne Bachleda

MAY NONE OF GOD'S WONDERFUL WORKS keep
silence, night or morning.
Bright stars, high mountains, the depths of the seas,
sources of rushing rivers:
May all these break into song as we sing to Father, Son,
and Holy Spirit.
May all the angels in the heavens reply:
Amen! Amen! Amen!
Power, praise, honor eternal glory to God, the only
Giver of grace.
Amen! Amen! Amen!

ANONYMOUS
a third-century doxology

 *Dawn*

THE DESERT BECOMES A PARADISE when it is accepted as desert. The desert can never be anything but a desert if we are trying to escape it. But once we fully accept it in union with the passion of Christ, it becomes a paradise. . . . This breakthrough into what you already have is only accomplished through the complete acceptance of the cross.

BROTHER DAVID STEINDL-RAST
from "Man of Prayer"
in *Thomas Merton, Monk: Monastic Tribute*

THROUGH DEATH immortality has come to all, and through the incarnation of the Word God's universal providence has been made known, together with him who is the giver and artificer of this providence, God the Word himself. For he became man that we might be made god; and he revealed himself through a body that we might receive an idea of the unseen Father; and he endured humiliation at men's hands that we might inherit incorruption. In himself he was in no way injured, for he is impassible and incorruptible, the very Word and God; but he endured these things for the sake of suffering men, and through his own impassibility he preserved and saved them. In short, the victories achieved by the Saviour through his incarnation are so great and so many that, if one wished to describe them it would be like gazing across the open sea and trying to count the waves.

St. Athanasius
fourth-century archbishop of Alexandria

Dusk

AS THOU HAST SET THE MOON IN THE SKY to be the poor man's lantern, so let thy Light shine in my dark life and lighten my path; as the rice is sown in the water and brings forth grain in great abundance, so let thy word be sown in our midst that the harvest may be great; and as the banyan sends forth its branches to take root in the soil, so let thy Life take root in our lives.

Anonymous Indian prayer

THE HAZELNUT

God showed me in my palm
a little thing round as a ball,
about the size of a hazelnut.
I looked at it with the eye of understanding
and asked myself:
"What is this thing?"
And I was answered:
"It is everything that is."
I wondered how it survived
since it seemed so little,
as though it could disintegrate in a second
into nothingness.
The answer came:
"It exists and always will exist,
because God loves it."
Just so does everything have being
because of God's love.

JULIAN OF NORWICH

 *Dawn*

LET MYSTERY HAVE ITS PLACE IN YOU; do not be always turning up your whole soil with the ploughshare of self-examination, but leave a little fallow corner in your heart ready for any seeds the wind may bring.

HENRI FREDERIC AMIEL

LORD GOD, we praise you for those riches of your
  creation which we shall never see:
for stars whose light will never reach the Earth;
for species of living things that were born,
that flourished and perished
before mankind appeared in the world;
for patterns and colors in the flowers,
which only insect eyes are able to see;
for strange, high music
that humans can never hear.
Lord God, you see everything that you have made and
  behold it is very good.

ANONYMOUS

Dusk

TO COMPREHEND YOUR AUDIBLE BREATH as the chambered wings of God's own heart rhythmically rising and falling in perpetuity . . . to perceive the sunset's lingering embrace on a friendly stranger's face as the star power burning in your own breast . . . to hold inside the light and power of the "single verse," the universe, . . . these are what walking in the woods will get you.

F. Lynne Bachleda

Dark

WHEN THE LAKE OF THE MIND becomes clear and still, man knows himself as he really is, always was, and always will be.

SWAMI PRABHAVANANDA
from *How to Know God*

THEREFORE I TELL YOU, do not worry about your life, what you will eat or what you will drink, or about your body, what you will wear. Is not life more than food, and the body more than clothing? Look at the birds of the air; they neither sow nor reap nor gather into barns, and yet your heavenly Father feeds them. Are you not of more value than they? And can any of you by worrying add a single hour to your span of life? And why do you worry about clothing? Consider the lilies of the field, how they grow; they neither toil nor spin, yet I tell you, even Solomon in all his glory was not clothed like one of these. But if God so clothes the grass of the field, which is alive today and tomorrow is thrown into the oven, will he not much more clothe you—you of little faith? Therefore do not worry, saying, "What will we eat?" or "What will we drink?" or "What will we wear?" For it is the Gentiles who strive for all these things; and indeed your heavenly Father knows that you need all these things. But strive first for the kingdom of God and his righteousness, and all these things will be given to you as well.

Jesus
in the Gospel of Matthew 6:25–33

O GOD, Most Merciful and Most Compassionate, who has given life to many and loves all that you have made, give us the spirit of your own loving-kindness that we may show mercy to all helpless creatures. Especially we would pray for those which minister to our comfort, that they may be treated with tender hands, thankful hearts, and that we may discover you, our Creator, in all created things. Amen.

ANONYMOUS

 *Dusk*

I WAS A SECRET TREASURE, and I created the creatures in order that I might be known.

HADITH, A MUSLIM TEACHING AUTHORITY

RUINED BY YOUR BEAUTY

First, you cleansed me,
arriving as fire, as savage flood.

Next you tore me,
your panther tooth,
your lion claws,
limbs scattering like grass
in the garden of a great wind.

Then you made love to me,
night after night of unendurable
torment and passion.

Ruined by your beauty,
I have vanished,
fled into the nothingness
of who I am.

DOROTHY WALTERS
from *Unmasking the Rose: A Record of a Kundalini Initiation*

 *Dawn*

LORD JESUS CHRIST, you are the sun that always rises, but never sets. You are the source of all life, creating and sustaining every living thing. You are the source of all food, material and spiritual, nourishing us in both body and soul. You are the light that dispels the clouds of error and doubt, and goes before me every hour of the day, guiding my thoughts and my actions. May I walk in your light, be nourished by your food, be sustained by your mercy, and be warmed by your love.

ERASMUS, SIXTEENTH-CENTURY SCHOLAR

MY LORD is boundless as the sun and moon,
Lighting heaven and earth;
How then can I have concerns about what is to be?

from *Man'yoshu*
a collection of Japanese poems
from the fifth century to the seventh century

 *Dusk*

ABBOT LOT CAME TO ABBOT JOSEPH and said: "Father, to the limit of my ability, I keep my little rule, my little fast, my prayer, meditation, and contemplative silence; and to the limit of my ability, I work to cleanse my heart of thoughts; what more should I do?" The elder rose up in reply and stretched out his hand to heaven, and his fingers became like ten lamps of fire. He said: "Why not be utterly changed into fire?"

ANDREW HARVEY
from *Teachings of the Christian Mystics*

THE IMPORTANT THING is to not stop questioning. Curiosity has its own reason for existing. One cannot help but be in awe when one contemplates the mysteries of eternity, of life, of the marvelous structure of reality. It is enough if one tries merely to comprehend a little of this mystery every day.

ALBERT EINSTEIN

 *Dawn*

NO CREATURE HAS MEANING without the Word of God. God's Word is in all creation, visible and invisible. The Word is living, being, spirit, all verdant greening, all creativity. This Word flashes out in every creature. This is how the spirit is in the flesh—the Word is indivisible from God.

ANDREW HARVEY
from *Teachings of the Christian Mystics*

MY HEART LEAPS UP WHEN I BEHOLD

My heart leaps up when I behold
   A rainbow in the sky:
So it was when my life began;
So is it now I am a man;
So be it when I shall grow old,
   Or let me die!
The Child is father of the Man:
And I could wish my days to be
Bound each to each by natural piety.

WILLIAM WORDSWORTH

 *Dusk*

THE LIVING OF LIFE, any life, involves great and private pain, much of which we share with no one. In such places as the Inner Gorge [of the Grand Canyon] the pain trails away from us. It is not so quiet there or so removed that you can hear yourself think, that you would even wish to; that comes later. You can hear your heart beat. That comes first.

BARRY LOPEZ
from "Gone Back into the Earth" in *Crossing Open Ground*

COMMUNING WITH GOD is communing with our own hearts, our own best selves, not with something foreign and accidental. Saints and devotees have gone into the wilderness to find God; of course they took God with them, and the silence and detachment enabled them to hear the still, small voice of their own souls, as one hears the ticking of his own watch in the stillness of the night. We are not cut off, we are not isolated points; the great currents flow through us and over us and around us and unite us to the whole of nature. Moses saw God in the burning bush, saw him with the eyes of early man whose divinities were clothed in the extraordinary, the fearful, or the terrible; we see him in the meanest weed that grows and hear him in the gentle murmur of our own heart's blood.

JOHN BURROUGHS
from *Accepting the Universe: The Faith of a Naturalist*

 *Dawn*

I REMEMBER SITTING day after day at the same table in a dull restaurant where I had to eat my lunch. There was a beautiful red rose in a small vase in the middle of the table. I looked at the rose with sympathy and enjoyed its beauty. Every day I talked with my rose. But then I became suspicious. Because while my mood was changing during the week from happy to sad, from disappointed to angry, from energetic to apathetic, my rose was always the same. And moved by my suspicion I lifted my fingers to the rose and touched it. It was a plastic thing. I was deeply offended and never went back there to eat.

We cannot talk with plastic nature because it cannot tell us the real story about life and death. But if we are sensitive to the voice of nature, we might be able to hear sounds from a world where man and nature both find their shape. We will never fully understand the meaning of the sacramental signs of bread and wine when they do not make us realize that the whole of nature is a sacrament pointing to a reality far beyond itself.

HENRI J. M. NOUWEN
from "Nature as a Sacramental Pointer" in *Creative Ministry*

I AM THE TRUE VINE, and my Father is the vinegrower. He removes every branch in me that bears no fruit. Every branch that bears fruit he prunes to make it bear more fruit. You have already been cleansed by the word that I have spoken to you. Abide in me as I abide in you. Just as the branch cannot bear fruit by itself unless it abides in the vine, neither can you unless you abide in me. I am the vine, you are the branches. Those who abide in me and I in them bear much fruit, because apart from me you can do nothing. Whoever does not abide in me is thrown away like a branch and withers; such branches are gathered, thrown into the fire, and burned. If you abide in me, and my words abide in you, ask for whatever you wish, and it will be done for you. My Father is glorified by this, that you bear much fruit and become my disciples.

As the Father has loved me, so I have loved you; abide in my love. If you keep my commandments, you will abide in my love, just as I have kept my Father's commandments and abide in his love. I have said these things to you so that my joy may be in you, and that your joy may be complete.

JESUS
in the Gospel of John 15:1–11

 *Dusk*

IT IS A BEAUTEOUS EVENING, CALM AND FREE

It is a beauteous evening, calm and free,
The holy time is quiet as a Nun
Breathless with adoration; the broad sun
Is sinking down in its tranquillity;
The gentleness of heaven broods o'er the Sea:
Listen! the mighty Being is awake,
And doth with his eternal motion make
A sound like thunder—everlastingly.
Dear Child! dear Girl! that walkest with me here,
If thou appear untouched by solemn thought,
Thy nature is not therefore less divine:
Thou liest in Abraham's bosom all the year;
And worship'st at the Temple's inner shrine,
God being with thee when we know it not.

WILLIAM WORDSWORTH

36

PEACE BE TO EARTH and to airy spaces.
Peace be to heaven, peace to the waters,
Peace to the plants and peace to the trees!
May all the gods grant me peace!
By this invocation of peace may peace be diffused!
By this invocation of peace may peace bring peace!
With this peace the dreadful I appease.
With this peace all evil I appease,
So that peace may prevail, happiness prevail!
May everything for us be peaceful!

from Atharva Veda

 *Dawn*

WE PRAY, LORD, for the humble beasts who with us bear the burden and heat of the day, giving their lives for the well-being of their countries; and for the wild creatures, whom you have made wise, strong, and beautiful; we ask for them your great tenderness of heart, for you have promised to save both man and beast, and great is your loving-kindness, O Savior of the world.

Anonymous Russian prayer

LISTENING

My father could hear a little animal step,
or a moth in the dark against the screen,
and every far sound called the listening out
into places where the rest of us had never been.

More spoke to him from the soft wild night
than came to our porch for us on the wind;
we would watch him look up and his face go keen
till the walls of the world flared, widened.

My father heard so much that we still stand
inviting the quiet by turning the face,
waiting for a time when something in the night
will touch us too from that other place.

WILLIAM STAFFORD
from *Stories That Could Be True*

LOVING GOD, who sees in us nothing that you have not given yourself, make my body healthy and agile, my mind sharp and clear, my heart joyful and contented, my soul faithful and loving. And surround me with the company of men and angels who share my devotion to you.

Above all, let me live in your presence, for with you all fear is banished, and there is only harmony and peace. Let every day combine the beauty of spring, the brightness of summer, the abundance of autumn, and the repose of winter. And at the end of my life on earth, grant that I may come to see and to know you in the fullness of your glory. Amen.

St. Thomas Aquinas

GOD DOES NOT LOOK at the caterpillar we are now, but the dazzling butterfly we have it in us to become.

BISHOP DESMOND TUTU
from *An African Prayer Book*

 *Dawn*

LIFT AN EARTHWORM from the freezing pavement to the soft, wet earth; car-cripple a doe in the same day. The wheel of life, the juxtaposition of improbable events, spins us ever outward. It is sleep that gives us rest, as much as food or air or water, that holds the rim from chaos to let our center be still.

F. LYNNE BACHLEDA

THE CANTICLE OF THE CREATURES

Most High, all-powerful, good Lord, yours are the
praises, the glory, the honor, and all blessing. To you
alone, Most High, do they belong, and no human is
worthy to mention your name.

Praised be you, my Lord, with all your creatures, above
all Brother Sun, who is the day and through whom
you give us light. He is beautiful and radiant with
great splendor; and bears a likeness of you, Most
High One.

Praised be you, my Lord, through Sister Moon and the
stars, in heaven you formed them clear and precious
and beautiful.

Praised be you, my Lord, through Brother Wind, and
through the air, cloudy and serene, and every kind of
weather through which you cherish your creatures.

Praised be you, my Lord, through Sister Water, which is
very useful and humble and precious and chaste.

Praised be you, my Lord, through Brother Fire, through
whom you light the night, and he is beautiful and
playful and robust and strong.

Praised be you, my Lord, through our Sister Mother
Earth, who sustains and governs us, and who pro-
duces varied fruits with colored flowers and herbs.
Praised be you, my Lord, through those who forgive in
your love and bear sickness and difficulty.
Blessed are those who endure in peace for by you, Most
High, they shall be crowned.
Praised be you, my Lord, through our Sister Bodily
Death, from whom no living man can escape.
Woe to those who die in mortal sin. Blessed are those
in death found obedient to your most holy will, for
death shall do them no harm.
Praise and bless my Lord and give him thanks and
serve him with great humility.

ST. FRANCIS OF ASSISI

LET NOT THE BLESSINGS we receive daily from God make us not to value or not to praise him because they be common; let us not forget to praise him for the innocent mirth and pleasure we have met with since we met together. What would a blind man give to see the pleasant rivers and meadows and flowers and fountains that we have met since we met thee, together!

I have been told, that if a man that was born blind could obtain to have his sight for only one hour during his whole life and should, at the first opening of his eyes, fix his sight upon the sun when it was in its full glory, either at rising or setting of it, he would be transported and amazed and so admire the glory of it that he would not willingly turn his eyes from that first ravishing object to behold all the other various beauties this world could present to him.

And this, and many other like blessings, we enjoy daily; and for most of them, because they are so common, most men forget to pay their praises, but let not us, because it is a sacrifice so pleasing to him that made the sun and us; and still protects us; and gives us flowers and showers, and stomachs and meat, and content, and leisure to go a-fishing.

Izaak Walton

Dark

TWO THINGS CONTINUE to fill the mind with ever-increasing awe and admiration: the starry heavens above and the moral law within.

IMMANUEL KANT
from *Critique of Pure Reason*

 *Dawn*

IT IS THE NATURE OF GOD to reside in mystery—ineluctable, inexhaustible mystery. We do not need to understand the cabala of mathematical physics to apprehend the *mysterium tremendum.* We need only look out the window.

CHET RAYMO
from *Skeptics and True Believers*

I DON'T USUALLY LIKE SEEING WILDLIFE from a plane very much: It's often the easiest way to see rare creatures, but it's not an intimate way to see them. With the condors, however, the experience in the plane was building into something remarkably different. I was with them in their element. In the air, they weren't cumbersome. They were at home. . . .

In the air, the condors had another culture, built on winds and air and wings. Next to us, [the condor] cruised on giant wings, body immobile, steady and strong. The feathers at the tips of his wings blew and fluttered as he glided through the air. His head swiveled, the way a modern dancer isolates and moves a single body part. I looked out of the plane window, watching his red head rotate while he flew, looking below, looking sideways. And looking straight at me.

There's nothing like being transfixed in the gaze of a spectacular wild animal. Always it's a shock to me—the sudden recognition of strangeness. In the condor's stare, I felt a disorienting self-consciousness that came with losing my role for a precious moment: I was no longer sure whether I was the seer or the seen. I got a fleeting sense of what I must look like to the condor, both of us made visible in the same light of day. The gaze also forced me to enter the picture, to occupy a place in the skies with the condor. In the look of the condor, I recognized a part of me that had existed unknown to myself.

I could also see in the look that the condor has a world and a life of its own, that it will always be strange to us. This was the condor of the skies, a magnificent soarer, looking down upon the monotonous and endless traffic of our lives.

CHARLES BERGMAN
from *Wild Echoes: Encounters with the Most Endangered Animals in North America*

FOR THE BEAUTY OF THE EARTH,
For the beauty of the skies,
For the love which from our birth
Over and around us lies:
Christ, our God, to thee we raise
This our sacrifice of praise.

For the beauty of each hour
Of the day and of the night,
Hill and vale and tree and flower,
Sun and moon and stars of light:
Christ, our God, to thee we raise
This our sacrifice of praise.

FOLLIOT SANDFORD PIERPOINT

 *Dark*

BY YOUR STRENGTH you established the mountains;
    you are girded with might.
You silence the roaring of the seas,
    the roaring of their waves,
    the tumult of the peoples.
Those who live at earth's farthest bounds are awed by
    your signs;
you make the gateways of the morning and the evening
    shout for joy.

You visit the earth and water it,
    you greatly enrich it;
the river of God is full of water;
    you provide the people with grain,
    for so you have prepared it.
You water its furrows abundantly,
    settling its ridges,
softening it with showers,
    and blessing its growth.
You crown the year with your bounty;
    your wagon tracks overflow with richness.
The pastures of the wilderness overflow,
    the hills gird themselves with joy,

The meadows clothe themselves with flocks,
  the valleys deck themselves with grain,
  they shout and sing together for joy.

KING DAVID
Psalm 65:6–13

 *Dawn*

THE FINAL MYSTERY IS ONESELF. When one has weighed the sun in the balance, and measured the steps of the moon, and mapped out the seven heavens star by star, there still remains oneself. Who can calculate the orbit of his own soul?

OSCAR WILDE
from *De Profundis*

GLORIOUS LORD CHRIST: the divine influence secretly diffused and active in the depths of matter, and the dazzling center where all the innumerable fibers of the manifold meet; power as implacable as the world and as warm as life; you whose forehead is of the whiteness of snow, whose eyes are of fire, and whose feet are brighter than molten gold; you whose hands imprison the stars; you who are the first and the last, the living and the dead and the risen again; you who gather into your exuberant unity every beauty, every affinity every energy, every mode of existence; it is you to whom my being cried out with a desire as vast as the universe, "In truth you are my Lord and my God."

PIERRE TEILHARD DE CHARDIN
from "Mass on the Altar of the World: Prayer"
in *Hymn of the Universe*

 *Dusk*

AND THE SUN GOES DOWN in waves of ether
in such a way that I can't tell if the day is ending, or the
   world,
or if the secret of secrets is inside me again.

ANNA AKHMATOVA
from *One Hundred Daffodils,* translated by Jane Kenyon

WHEN I HEARD THE LEARN'D ASTRONOMER

When I heard the learn'd astronomer,
When the proofs, the figures were arranged in columns
  before me,
When I was shown the charts and diagrams, to add,
divide, and measure them,
When I sitting heard the astronomer where he lectured
With much applause in the lecture-room,
How soon unaccountable I became tired and sick,
Till rising and gliding out I wander'd off by myself
In the mystical moist night-air and from time to time,
Look'd up in perfect silence at the stars.

WALT WHITMAN

 *Dawn*

AND GOD SAID TO THE SOUL:
I desired you before the world began.
I desire you now
As you desire me.
And where the desires of two come together
There love is perfected.

How the Soul Speaks to God
Lord, you are my lover,
My longing,
My flowing stream,
My sun,
And I am your reflection.

How God Answers the Soul
It is my nature that makes me love you often,
For I am love itself
It is my longing that makes me love you intensely,
For I yearn to be loved from the heart.
It is my eternity that makes me love you long,
For I have no end.

Mechthild of Magdeburg
from *Teachings of the Christian Mystics*

WE THANK THEE, LORD, for the glory of the late days and the excellent face of thy sun. We thank thee for good news received. We thank thee for the pleasures we have enjoyed and for those we have been able to confer. And now, when the clouds gather and rain impends over the forest and our house, permit us not to be cast down; let us not lose the savor of past mercies and past pleasures; but, like the voice of a bird singing in the rain, let grateful memory survive in the hour of darkness.

ROBERT LOUIS STEVENSON

 *Dusk*

SILENTLY SMOKE SEEPS INTO US,
whispering long after the mesmerizing blaze:
"Remember my fire,"
our perceptions caressed
by God's lingering perfume.

F. LYNNE BACHLEDA

LORD JESUS CHRIST, you are the gentle moon and joyful stars that watch over the darkest night. You are the source of all peace, reconciling the whole universe to the Father. You are the source of all rest, calming troubled hearts and bringing sleep to weary bodies. You are the sweetness that fills our minds with quiet joy and can turn the worst nightmares into dreams of heaven. May I dream of your sweetness, rest in your arms, be at one with your Father, and be comforted in the knowledge that you always watch over me.

ERASMUS, SIXTEENTH-CENTURY SCHOLAR

 *Dawn*

WE THANK THEE

For mother-love and father-care,
For brothers strong and sisters fair,
For love at home and here each day,
For guidance lest we go astray,

Father in Heaven, we thank Thee.

For this new morning with its light,
For rest and shelter of the night,
For health and food, for love and friends,
For everything His goodness sends,

Father in Heaven, we thank Thee.

For flowers that bloom about our feet,
For tender grass, so fresh, so sweet,
For song of bird and hum of bee,
For all things fair we hear or see,

Father in Heaven, we thank Thee.

For blue of stream and blue of sky,
For pleasant shade of branches high,
For fragrant air and cooling breeze,
For beauty of the blooming trees,

Father in Heaven, we thank Thee.

RALPH WALDO EMERSON

○ *Day*

I MUST SHARE WITH YOU a story about a particularly barren time in my life when I used a tree for a spiritual director. I learned so much that year because I listened in silence. . . .

Because it was small I couldn't lean on it but could only sit beside it. That taught me a lot about what the role of spiritual guide should be.

Even though it was small, it had the ability to give me a certain amount of shade. You don't have to have a lot of leaves to give shade.

Because it was silent I listened deeply. You don't need a lot of words to connect with God.

When it got thirsty I watered it. The miracle of water is a little like the miracle of God's love. That little sycamore taught me a lot about foot washing. Watering it was a great joy. A soul–friend relationship never works only one way. There is a mutual giving and receiving.

I learned from my tree that being transplanted is possible. I can always put down roots again, connect with the Great Root, and grow on. . . .

I wouldn't recommend using a tree for a spiritual guide all the days of one's life, but that sycamore got me through a long stretch of barrenness. It was only a little tree, and I didn't know it was holy until I spent time with it. Truly, holiness comes wrapped in the ordinary.

Sister Macrina Wiederkehr
from *A Tree Full of Angels*

 *Dusk*

THE ANIMALS

They do not live in the world,
Are not in time and space,
From birth to death hurled
No word do they have, not one
To plant a foot upon,
Were never in any place.

For by words the world was called
Out of the empty air,
With words was shaped and walled
Line and circle and square,
Mud and emerald,
Snatched from deceiving death
By the articulate breath.

But these have never trod
Twice the familiar track,
Never never turned back
Into the memoried day;
All is new and near
In the unchanging Here

Of the fifth great day of God,
That shall remain the same,
Never shall pass away.

On the sixth day we came.

EDWIN MUIR

 *Dark*

NOW MAY EVERY LIVING THING, young or old, weak or strong, living near or far, known or unknown, living or departed or yet unborn, may every living thing be full of bliss.

BUDDHA

Dawn ☼

BY PERSONALITY, intuition, or will, sometimes in nature I try too hard and in vain to squeeze the divine out of every ubiquitous blade of grass, every common grasshopper, every fat, skittish water snake, every gently menacing distant strobe of summer lightning. This is a misapplication of effort, I think. More like the air born into us as storm, breeze, or swelter, entering our core through the natural world, we always have God's mercy whether we know it or not. As in breathing without concentrating on this miracle, the rescue of beauty, texture, sound, heat, and light saturates and saves us, whether we know it or not.

F. LYNNE BACHLEDA

Day

TO SEE A WORLD in a grain of sand
And a heaven in a wild flower,
Hold infinity in the palm of your hand
And eternity in an hour. . . .

The bat that flits at close of eve
Has left the brain that won't believe.
The owl that calls upon the night
Speaks the unbeliever's fright. . . .

The bleat, the bark, bellow, and roar
Are waves that beat on heaven's shore. . . .

If the sun and moon should doubt,
They'd immediately go out. . . .

God appears, and God is light
To those poor souls who dwell in night,
But does a human form display
To those who dwell in realms of day.

WILLIAM BLAKE
from "Auguries of Innocence"

Dusk

THE WIND BLOWS WHERE IT CHOOSES, and you hear the sound of it, but you do not know where it comes from or where it goes. So it is with everyone who is born of the Spirit.

JESUS
in the Gospel of John 3:8

 *Dark*

THE SUBSTANCE OF THE WINDS is too thin for human eyes, their written language is too difficult for human minds, and their spoken language mostly too faint for the ears.

JOHN MUIR

Dawn ☼

AFTER YOU HAVE SOWN in the soil of Cosmic Consciousness your vibratory prayer-seed, do not pluck it out frequently to see whether or not it has germinated. Give the divine force a chance to work uninterruptedly.

PARAMAHANSA YOGANANDA
from *Scientific Healing Affirmations*

Day

SEED. There are so many beginnings. In Japan, I recall, there were wildflowers that grew in the far, cool region of mountains. The bricks of Hiroshima, down below, were formed of clay from these mountains, and so the walls of houses and shops held the dormant trumpet flower seeds. But after one group of humans killed another with the explosive power of life's smallest elements split wide apart, the mountain flowers began to grow. Out of the crumbled, burned buildings they sprouted. Out of destruction and bomb heat and the falling of walls, the seeds opened up and grew. What a horrible beauty, the world going its own way, growing without us. But perhaps this, too, speaks of survival, of hope beyond our time.

Linda Hogan
from *Dwellings: A Spiritual History of the Living World*

Dusk

THE DAY WILL COME WHEN, after harnessing the
ether, the winds, the tides, and gravitation, we shall har-
ness for God the energies of love. And, on that day, for
the second time in the history of the world, man will
have discovered fire.

PIERRE TEILHARD DE CHARDIN
from *Hymn of the Universe*

 *Dark*

GOD BEFORE ME, God behind me,
God above me, God below me;
I am on the path of God,
God upon my track.
Who is there on land?
Who is there on wave?
Who is there on billow?
Who is there by doorpost?
Who is there along with us?
God and Lord.
I am here abroad,
I am here in need,
I am here in pain,
I am here in straits,
I am here alone,
O God, aid me.

Anonymous Celtic prayer

WE NEED ANOTHER and a wiser and perhaps a more mystical concept of animals. Remote from universal nature, and living by complicated artifice, man in civilization surveys the creatures through the glass of his knowledge and sees thereby a feather magnified and the whole image in distortion. We patronize them for their incompleteness, for their tragic fate of having taken form so far below ourselves. And there we err, and greatly err. For the animal shall not be measured by man. In a world older and more complete than ours they move finished and complete, gifted with extensions of the senses we have lost and never attained, living by voices we shall never hear. They are not brethren; they are not underlings; they are other nations, caught with ourselves in the net of life and time, fellow prisoners of the splendor and travail of the earth.

HENRY BESTON
from *The Outermost House: A Year of Life
on the Great Beach of Cape Cod*

Day

ONE AFTERNOON as the children watched television and I folded laundry, we heard a terrible thud against the patio door. I turned in time to see blue wings falling to the ground. A bird had flown into the glass.

None of us said a word. We looked at one another and crept to the door. The children followed me outside. I half-expected the bird to be dead, but she wasn't. She was stunned and her right wing was a little lopsided, but it didn't look broken—bruised, maybe.

The bird sat perfectly still, her eyes tiny and afraid. She looked so fragile and alone that I sat down beside her. I reached out my little finger and brushed her wing.

A voice came from behind me. "Why doesn't it fly off, Mama?"

"She's hurt," I said. "She just needs to be still."

We watched her. We watched her stillness. Finally the children wandered back to the television, satisfied that nothing was going to "happen" for a while. But I couldn't leave her.

I sat beside her, unable to resist the feeling that we shared something, the two of us. The wounds and broken-ness of life. Crumpled wings. A collision with something harsh and real. I felt like crying for her. For myself. For every broken thing in the world.

That moment taught me that while the postures of stillness within the cocoon are frequently an individual experience, we also need to share our stillness. The bird taught me anew that we're all in this together, that we need to sit in one another's stillness and take up corporate postures of prayer. How wonderful it is when we can be honest and free enough to say to one another, "I need you to wait with me," or "Would you like me to wait with you?"

I studied the bird, deeply impressed that she seemed to know instinctively that in stillness is healing. I had been learning that too, learning that stillness can be the prayer that transforms us. How much more concentrated our stillness becomes, though, when it's shared.

The door opened again. "Is she finished being still yet?"

"No, not yet," I said, knowing that I was talking as much about myself as the bird. We went on waiting together. Twenty minutes. Thirty. Fifty.

Finally she was finished being still. She cocked her head to one side, lifted her wings, and flew. The sight of her flying made me catch my breath. From the corner of my eye I saw her shadow move along the ground and cross over me. Grace is everywhere, I thought. Then I picked myself up and went back to folding laundry.

SUE MONK KIDD
from *When the Heart Waits*

WE HUMANS THINK WE ARE SMART, but an orchid, for example, knows how to produce noble, symmetrical flowers, and a snail knows how to make a beautiful, well-proportioned shell. Compared with their knowledge, ours is not worth much at all. We should bow deeply before the orchid and the snail and join our palms reverently before the monarch butterfly and the magnolia tree. The feeling of respect for all species will help us recognize the noblest nature in ourselves.

THICH NHAT HANH
from *Love in Action: Writings on Nonviolent Social Change*

 *Dark*

AH, NOT TO BE CUT OFF,
not through the slightest partition
shut out from the law of the stars.
The inner—what is it?
if not intensified sky,
hurled through with birds and deep
with the winds of homecoming.

RAINER MARIA RILKE
from *The Enlightened Heart*

I ASK ALL BLESSINGS,
I ask them with reverence,
of my mother the earth,
of the sky, moon, and sun my father.
I am old age: the essence of life,
I am the source of all happiness.
All is peaceful, all in beauty,
all in harmony, all in joy.

ANONYMOUS NAVAHO PRAYER

Day

TODAY, in the opening years of the twenty-first century, we find ourselves in a critical moment when the religious traditions need to awaken again to the natural world as the primary manifestation of the divine to human intelligence. The very nature and purpose of the human is to experience this intimate presence that comes to us through natural phenomena. Such is the purpose of having eyes and ears and feeling sensitivity, and all our other senses. We have no inner spiritual development without outer experience. Immediately, when we see or experience any natural phenomenon, when we see a flower, a butterfly, a tree, when we feel the evening breeze flow over us or wade in a stream of clear water, our natural response is immediate, intuitive, transforming, ecstatic. Everywhere we find ourselves invaded by the world of the sacred.

THOMAS BERRY
from the introduction to *When the Trees Say Nothing:*
Writings on Nature by Thomas Merton

LORD, JUST AS DAY DECLINES TO EVENING, so often after some little pleasure my heart declines into depression. Everything seems dull and every action feels like a burden. If anyone speaks, I scarcely listen. If anyone knocks, I scarcely hear. My heart is as hard as flint. Then I go out into the field to meditate, to read the holy Scriptures; and I write down my deepest thoughts in a letter to you. And suddenly your grace, dear Jesus, shatters the darkness with daylight, lifts the burden, relieves the tension. Soon tears follow sighs, and with those tears heavenly joy floods over me.

AELRED OF RIEVAULX
from "Healing at Dusk"

Dark

THIS UNIVERSE would never have been suitably put together into one form from such various and opposite parts, unless there were some One who joined such different parts together; and when joined, the very variety of their natures, so discordant among themselves, would break their harmony and tear them asunder unless the One held together what it wove into one whole. Such a fixed order of nature could not continue its course, could not develop motions taking such various directions in place, time, operation, space, and attributes, unless there were One who, being immutable, had the disposal of these various changes. And this cause of their remaining fixed and their moving, I call God, according to the name familiar to all.

ANICIUS MANLIUS SEVERINUS BOETHIUS
SIXTH-CENTURY ROMAN STATESMAN AND PHILOSOPHER
from *The Consolation of Philosophy,*
which he wrote while imprisoned for heresy

Dawn

MAY THE ROAD RISE TO MEET YOU.

May the wind be always at your back.

May the sun shine warm upon your face.

May the rains fall softly upon your fields.

And until we meet again, may God hold you in the
    hollow of his hand.

ANONYMOUS GAELIC BLESSING

Day

DURING MY LIFE, throughout my entire life little by little, the world has become ignited, inflamed to my eyes until, all around me, it has become entirely illuminated from within . . . so much so that when I touched the ground, I experienced the Divine Transparence at the heart of a universe that has become ablaze.

PIERRE TEILHARD DE CHARDIN
from "Mass on the Altar of the World" in *Hymn of the Universe*

"**SEE YONDER THERE**—that's my friend," he said.

"The fire?" asked Nell the child.

"It has been alive as long as I have. We talk and think together. . . . It's like a book to me, and many an old story it tells me. It's music, for I should know its voice among a thousand, and there are other voices in its roar. It has its pictures too. You don't know how many strange faces and different scenes I trace in the red-hot coals. It's my memory, that fire, and shows me all my life."

CHARLES DICKENS
from *The Old Curiosity Shop*

 *Dark*

THAT WHICH OFFERS ITSELF to us with starlight,
that which offers itself to us,
hold it like world in your face with might,
take it seriously.

Show night that you received silently
what it bestowed on you.
Not until you go over to it entirely
will night know you.

RAINER MARIA RILKE
from "Magic" in *Rilke on Love and Other Difficulties*

EARTH, SKY, WORLDS ABOVE, quarters and their
　halves;
Fire, air, sun, moon, and stars; water, herbs, trees,
Space and entity are the elements.
Eye, ear, mind, tongue, and touch; skin, flesh, muscle.
Marrow and skeleton; and the five
Vital forces constitute the body.
The sage, contemplating these sets of five,
Discovered that everything is holy.
Man can complete the inner with the outer.

from Taittiriya Upanishad, translated by Eknath Easwaran

Day

IF I WERE ALONE in a desert where I was afraid, and if I had a child with me, my fear would disappear and I would be strengthened; so noble, so full of pleasure and so powerful is life in itself. If I could not keep a child with me, and if I had at least a live animal with me, I would be comforted. Therefore, let those who bring about great wonders in black books take an animal—perhaps a dog—to help them. The life within the animal will give them strength. Equality gives strength in all things.

MEISTER ECKHART
from *A Spirituality Named Compassion:
Uniting Mystical Awareness with Social Justice*

BLESS THE LORD, O my soul.

O LORD my God, you are very great.
You are clothed with honor and majesty,
   wrapped in light as with a garment.
You stretch out the heavens like a tent,
   you set the beams of your chambers on the waters,
you make the clouds your chariot,
   you ride on the wings of the wind,
you make the winds your messengers,
   fire and flame your ministers.

You set the earth on its foundations,
   so that it shall never be shaken.
You cover it with the deep as with a garment;
   the waters stood above the mountains.
At your rebuke they flee;
   at the sound of your thunder they take to flight.
They rose up to the mountains, ran down to the valleys
   to the place that you appointed for them.
You set a boundary that they may not pass,
   so that they might not again cover the earth.

You make springs gush forth in the valleys;
    they flow between the hills,
giving drink to every wild animal;
    the wild asses quench their thirst.
By the streams the birds of the air have their habitation;
    they sing among the branches.
From your lofty abode you water the mountains;
    the earth is satisfied with the fruit of your work.

You cause the grass to grow for the cattle,
    and plants for people to use,
to bring forth food from the earth,
    and wine to gladden the human heart,
oil to make the face shine,
    and bread to strengthen the human heart.
The trees of the LORD are watered abundantly,
    the cedars of Lebanon that he planted.
In them the birds build their nests;
    the stork has its home in the fir trees.
The high mountains are for the wild goats;
    the rocks are a refuge for the coneys.

You have made the moon to mark the seasons;
    the sun knows its time for setting.
You make darkness, and it is night,
    when all the animals of the forest come creeping out.
The young lions roar for their prey,
    seeking their food from God.
When the sun rises, they withdraw
    and lie down in their dens.
People go out to their work
    and to their labor until the evening.

O Lord, how manifold are your works!
    In wisdom you have made them all;
    the earth is full of your creatures.

I will sing to the Lord as long as I live;
    I will sing praise to my God while I have being.

Psalm 104:1–25, 33

 Dark

---

ETERNAL EPHEMERAL,
I find you on earth
in sands that sift,
sink low in sea breeze;
changelings letting
go of their life
against the constant sea.

F. LYNNE BACHLEDA

Dawn ☀

WHEN JESUS COMMANDED people to "love their neighbor as themselves," did he say that all neighbors were necessarily two-legged ones?

Matthew Fox
from *A Spirituality Named Compassion:
Uniting Mystical Awareness with Social Justice*

Day

TODAY, MY FATHER, let me be like a tree planted by the river, bringing forth fruit in its season. Let the sap of your Holy Spirit rise within me. Let me not become dry and barren but rich in abundance and fertility. May many weary ones find refreshment in the shadow of my branches.

BROTHER RAMÓN, S.S.F.

Dusk

THE FAITH AND COMPOSURE of the naturalist or naturist are proof against the worst that Nature can do. He sees the cosmic forces only; he sees nothing directly mindful of man, but man himself; he sees the intelligence and beneficence of the universe flowering in man; he sees life as a mysterious issue of the warring element; he sees human consciousness and our sense of right and wrong, of truth and justice, as arising in the evolutionary sequence, and turning and sitting in judgment upon all things; there can be no life without pain and death; that there can be no harmony without discord, that opposites go hand in hand; that good and evil are inextricably mingled; that the sun and blue sky are still there behind the clouds, unmindful of them; that all is right with the world if we extend our vision deep enough; that the ways of Nature are the ways of God if we do not make God in our own image, and make our comfort and well-being the prime object of Nature. Our comfort and well-being are provided for in the constitution of the world, but we may say that they are not guaranteed; they are contingent upon many things, but the chances are upon our side. He that would save his life shall lose it—lose it in forgetting that the universe is not a close corporation, or a patented article, and that it exists for other ends than our own. But he who can lose his life in the larger life of the whole shall save it in a deeper, truer sense.

JOHN BURROUGHS
from *Accepting the Universe: The Faith of a Naturalist*

Dark ●

OH! IN HIS RAPTURE he was weeping even over those stars, which were shining to him from the abyss of space, and he was not ashamed of that ecstasy. There seemed to be threads from all those innumerable worlds of God, linking his soul to them, and it was trembling all over in contact with other worlds.

FYODOR DOSTOYEVSKY
from *The Brothers Karamazov*

 *Dawn*

SINCE ONCE AGAIN, LORD—though this time not in the forests of the Aisne but in the steppes of Asia—I have neither bread, nor wine, nor altar, I will raise myself beyond these symbols, up to the pure majesty of the real itself; I, your priest, will make the whole earth my altar and on it will offer you all the labors and sufferings of the world.

Over there, on the horizon, the sun has just touched with light the outermost fringe of the eastern sky. Once again, beneath this moving sheet of fire, the living surface of the earth wakes and trembles and once again begins its fearful travail. I will place on my paten, O God, the harvest to be won by this renewal of labor. Into my chalice, I shall pour all the sap which is to be pressed out this day from the earth's fruits.

My paten and my chalice are the depths of a soul laid widely open to all the forces which in a moment will rise up from every corner of the earth and converge upon the Spirit. Grant me the remembrance and the mystic presence of all those whom the light is now awakening to the new day.

PIERRE TEILHARD DE CHARDIN
from "Mass on the Altar of the World: The Offering"
in *Hymn of the Universe*

A MILLION MIRACLES

O Son of God, perform a miracle for me: change my
heart. You, whose crimson blood redeems mankind,
whiten my heart.

It is you who makes the sun bright and the ice sparkle;
you who makes the rivers flow and the salmon leap.

Your skilled hand makes the nut tree blossom, and the
corn turn golden; your spirit composes the songs of
the birds and the buzz of the bees.

Your creation is a million wondrous miracles, beautiful
to behold. I ask of you just one more miracle: beautify
my soul.

Anonymous Irish prayer

Dusk

THE BIG STAR HAS RETIRED after a glorious day. Dragonflies swoop to navigate the lesser winds of a cooler sky. An anhinga, heron, or crane (so much has slipped with the tide) stands at the ready beside his old fisherman, the buddy who slipped him a whole fish. After pausing to savor his luck, the bird tossed it back like a shot of tequila. Their simple relationship dominates this patch of shore. The old man now oblivious, the creature devoted. Soft dianthus pink and slate and dusky green hold their bond.

> Saltwater sees home.
> Stirs itself to recognition,
> Surges well in my eyes, sure.

It's easy to tell the worshippers here. They visit all day. In this church frequency counts more than duration. Staring out at the simplest of compositions, *the* dominant design, we who know are still crawling out or trying to crawl back in. It's a lover's warmth or smiling voice. You know it exists without you, but your need is total and nonetheless.

Last light fades. The page glows, but not for long.
The breath of God still moves with power. Stirs these
waves and makes music in this haunting night.

F. LYNNE BACHLEDA

 *Dark*

NIGHT SILENCE

Lord of light
help me to know
that you are also
Lord of night.

And by your choice
when all is dark
and still and stark
you use your voice.

HARRY ALFRED WIGGETT

OUTSIDE THE CATHEDRAL holding ancient relics in Valencia, a woman kissed pigeons. She saw these birds as symbols of God. Gray and white and black as discarded shells, these were creatures I'd been taught to think of as "filthy." They *seemed* filthy, in fact, with their staring orange eyes and patchy feathers. But now, while I looked, they turned into doves. Of course they always were doves, or rather, of course doves always really were a type of pigeon. But I never really believed it until this woman showed me her belief. Her kiss transformed ugliness to beauty.

So it was like a fairy tale after all. It was the old story: what is loved reveals its loveliness. Here she squatted, radiant, smiling, enrobed in life, in a dozen pairs of folded wings, in a dozen pairs of pearl gray and, as I looked, yes, even lavender, even royal-purple wings—a woman in an ordinary black cotton dress who smiled as if she knew she was the luckiest person on earth, swathed in blessing.

BONNIE FRIEDMAN
from *Writing Past Dark*

Day

EVERY BEING HAS ITS OWN INTERIOR, its self, its mystery, its numinous aspect. To deprive any being of this sacred quality is to disrupt the total order of the universe. Reverence will be total, or it will not be at all. The universe does not come to us in pieces any more than a human individual stands before us with some part of his being.

THOMAS BERRY
from "The New Story: Comments on the Origin,
Identification, and Transmission of Values"

ALMIGHTY ONE, in the woods I am blessed.

Happy everyone in the woods.

Every tree speaks of thee.

O God! What glory in the woodland!

On the heights in peace—peace to serve him.

LUDWIG VAN BEETHOVEN

 *Dark*

GAINING ENLIGHTENMENT is like the moon reflecting in the water.
The moon does not get wet, nor is the water disturbed.
Although its light is extensive and great, the moon is
   reflected even in a puddle an inch across.
The whole moon and the whole sky are reflected in a
   dewdrop in the grass, in one drop of water.
Enlightenment does not disturb the person, just as the
   moon does not disturb the water.

Eihei Dogen, thirteenth-century Zen poet
from "The Way of Everyday Life"

Dawn ☀

THE KINGDOM OF HEAVEN is like a mustard seed that someone took and sowed in his field; it is the smallest of all the seeds, but when it has grown it is the greatest of shrubs and becomes a tree, so that the birds of the air come and make nests in its branches.

JESUS
in the Gospel of Matthew 13:31–32

Day

WE ARE THE SEED OF GOD. A pear seed grows into a pear tree; a hazel seed into a hazel tree; a seed of God into God.

MEISTER ECKHART
from *A Spirituality Named Compassion:*
Uniting Mystical Awareness with Social Justice

TWILIGHT

Spirit of Twilight, through your folded wings
I catch a glimpse of your averted face,
And rapturous on a sudden, my soul sings
"Is not this common earth a holy place?"

Spirit of Twilight, you are like a song
That sleeps, and waits a singer, like a hymn
That God finds lovely and keeps near him long,
Till it is choired by aureoled cherubim.

Spirit of Twilight, in the golden gloom
Of dreamland dim I sought you, and I found
A woman sitting in a silent room
Full of white flowers that moved and made no sound.

These white flowers were the thoughts you bring to all,
And the room's name is Mystery where you sit,
Woman whom we call Twilight, when night's pall
You lift across our Earth to cover it.

OLIVE CUSTANCE

 Dark

SURELY I KNOW THE SPRING THAT SWIFTLY FLOWS

Surely I know the spring that swiftly flows
even during the night.

The eternal spring is deeply hidden,
but surely I know the place where it begins
even during the night.

I don't know its source because it has none
but know that all beginnings come from this one,
even during the night.

I do know that nothing can equal its beauty
and that from it both heaven and earth drink
even during the night.

I know there is no limit to its depth
and that no one can wade across its breadth
even during the night.

Its brightness is never clouded over,
and I know that from it all light flows,
even during the night,

I know its current is so forceful
that it floods the nations, heaven, and hell,
even during the night.

The current that is born of this stream,
I know, is swift and overpowering,
even during the night.

As for the current that flows from these two,
I know that neither one comes before it,
even during the night.

The eternal stream is deeply hidden
in this living bread, to give us life,
even during the night.

Here the call goes out to the creatures,
and they drink their fill, though in the dark,
because it is at night.

This living stream that I so desire,
I see it in this bread of life,
even during the night.

ST. JOHN OF THE CROSS
translated by Ken Krabbenhoft

Dawn

IT IS NECESSARY FOR ME TO SEE the first point of light which begins to be dawn. It is necessary to be present alone at the resurrection of Day, in the solemn silence at which the sun appears, for at this moment all the affairs of cities, of governments, of war departments, are seen to be the bickerings of mice. I receive from the Eastern woods, the tall oaks, the one word *day*, which is never the same. It is always in a totally new language.

Thomas Merton
from *Dancing in the Water of Life: Seeking Peace in the Hermitage*

Day

THE CREATOR

Creator of all people, who made what exists!
Who made grass for the herds,
The life-bearing trees for humans;
Who permits the fish to live in the river,
The birds to touch the sky.
You sustain the grasshopper
And keep alive even the gnat,
The creeping and the flying things alike;
Who made food for the mice in their holes
And feed the flying creatures on every tree.

Hail to you for all these things!
The one, the only one, with many hands,
Who lies awake for all people when they sleep,
Seeking what is best for his animals!

Ancient Egyptian hymn

WHEN THE WASH TIGHTENED INTO BEDROCK I found Dry 001[1]. It held about sixteen gallons of clear water. I stood for a moment in front of it, trying not to act desperate or crazily excited. I simply stared at the water, letting my hands list to my sides. I drank, taking water from just beneath the surface, then made notes and measurements, spanning a tape measure across the surface and then to the bottom. The hole was the shape of a cone, so I calculated the volume based on the volume of a cone. Not too accurate, but good enough. The name for a water hole like this is *tinaja,* Spanish for "earthen jar," a description I have always liked. A person who constructs or sells water jars is a *tinajero.* The English word often used as a parallel is *tank,* not nearly as rich or descriptive a term.

I gathered a couple of gallons from the *tinaja.* A gift. I tried to take this with my head down, and I worried that my disinterested taking of measurements might not be the proper response to something giving me life. I

---

[1] A desert suryveyor's designation for a water hole.

paused there thinking of how I should act, what words I should use. Nothing came. The desert is full of simple acts with indescribable significance.

CRAIG CHILDS
from *The Secret Knowledge of Water*

THE SUN AND THE STARS SHINING glorify God. They stand where he placed them, they move where he bid them. "The heavens declare the glory of God." They glorify God, but they do not know it. The birds sing to him, the thunder speaks of his terror, the lion is like his strength, the sea is like his greatness, the honey like his sweetness; they are something like him, they make him known, they tell of him, they give him glory, but they do not know they do.

GERARD MANLEY HOPKINS
from "The Principal or Foundation," an address based on the
opening of St. Ignatius of Loyola's *Spiritual Exercises*

 *Dawn*

DON'T MAKE LISTS

Every day a new flower rises
from your body's fresh soil.
Don't go around looking
for fallen petals
in a fairy tale, when you've
got the golden plant
right here, now,
shooting forth in light from your eyes,
your awakening crown.

Don't make lists, or explore ancient accounts.
Forget everything you know
and open.

DOROTHY WALTERS
from *Marrow of Flame: Poems of the Spiritual Journey*

Day

THINKING ABOUT ELDERS led me to think about birth order. Whether you hold with the Bible or with Darwin's story of the world, we all agree that humans appeared last on the scene. We're all familiar with the idea that if the celebration of life on earth was contained in a single day, human beings would have arrived at the party but a few moments before midnight. We may have big brains, but we are the baby of the family. Let's set aside semantic play about "dominion over the earth." What if there is something quite simple at work in this fact of birth order? In a direct way I think we need, biologically and metaphysically, the all of creation that preceded us and that predicated the all that now surrounds us.

Of course I need rivers for my drinking water and corn for food. Of course I need trees for my "stick-built" house, air for my lungs, and for life itself, the sun. But I am advancing the idea that although the bluebirds appear to be not so critical to my survival, more than I fathom, I less palpably and mysteriously need them, too. I might also really require to see the stars that sweep my Milky Way; might also really crave the caress and power of the wind; might rely on the growl of wild animals; might need the shock of fuschia a flower affords; and might hunger for the infinite flavors of wildness and blessings that this world affords me. If we allow that the divine is truly within all creation, is "catholic in nature," then these needs and their complementary satisfactions make sense. Then we have spiritual requirements that can be met with great ease. Outside God is always within sight and earshot, at our fingers, on the tips of our tongues, and in the fragrances that transport us to portals old and new. Let us partake of this all-encompassing communion.

F. Lynne Bachleda

IF YOU WISH TO KNOW THE DIVINE, feel the wind on your face and the warm sun on your hand.

BUDDHA

 *Dark*

THE STARS SHINE

O Lord, the stars shine
and men's eyes are closed.
The doors of kings are shut
and lovers behold their beloved.
Here I am, alone with you.

RABIA AL-ADAWIYYA

CHRIST IS ALREADY IN THE MIDST of all the poor things of this earth, which we cannot leave because it is our mother. He is in the expectation of all creatures, which without knowing it, wait to share in the glorification of his body. He is in the history of the earth, the blind course of which in all victories and all breakdowns is moving with uncanny precision toward his day, the day on which his glory, transforming all things, will break forth from its own depths. He is in all tears and in all death as hidden rejoicing and as the life which triumphs by appearing to die. . . . He is there as the most secret law and the innermost essence of all things which still triumphs and prevails even when all order and structure seem to be disintegrating.

He is with us like the light of day and the air which we do not notice, like the hidden law of a movement which we do not grasp, because the part which we ourselves experience is too short for us to discern the formula of the movement. But he is there, the heart of this earthly world and the secret seal of its eternal validity.

Consequently, we children of this earth may love it, must love it.

Karl Rahner
from *The Great Church Year*

VERY TRULY, I TELL YOU, unless a grain of wheat falls into the earth and dies, it remains just a single grain; but if it dies, it bears much fruit.

JESUS
in the Gospel of John 12:24

 *Dusk*

SINCE WE FIRST THOUGHT to worship anything, what points to the immanent power of the Universe that we worship in common? Of course, it must have been the wonder of the natural world that first drew us out of ourselves, a haunting call like geese in a darkening gray winter sky. Collectively they say, "This way, together, toward warmth, safety, and a sense of what can be and what's to come."

F. Lynne Bachleda

THE MOON

I see the moon,
And the moon sees me;
God bless the moon,
And God bless me.

Anonymous Celtic children's rhyme

 *Dawn*

WHO CANNOT BE CAUGHT UP by the form of a seagull in flight, by the straight back of a proud dog, by the graceful strides of a tiger, by the perfect musculature of a fine stallion? Beauty is not an appendage to human and spiritual living but of its very essence. Animals are here in part to grant glimpses of the grace of beauty. The beauty of the singing of birds is a kind of music in itself, as is the gurgling of a brook, the dashing of ocean waves against a rocky shore, the whistling of the wind among leafy trees. . . . Animals have a sense of their own worth and dignity—a pride at their own unique existence that subtly suggests that no one ever preached to them about original sin. As a result they appear at home with silence, with themselves, and with solitude. I have been amazed in recent years to learn how many animals come out to watch the sun set, for example. Ducks, birds, dogs, and God knows how many smaller creatures have a contemplative side to them that the human species of late has all but forgotten.

MATTHEW FOX
from *A Spirituality Named Compassion:*
Uniting Mystical Awareness with Social Justice

JOYFUL, JOYFUL, WE ADORE THEE

Joyful, joyful, we adore Thee, God of glory, Lord of
 love;
Hearts unfold like flowers before Thee, opening to the
 sun above.
Melt the clouds of sin and sadness; drive the dark of
 doubt away;
Giver of immortal gladness, fill us with the light of day!

All Thy works with joy surround Thee; earth and heaven
 reflect Thy rays;
Stars and angels sing around Thee, center of unbroken
 praise.
Field and forest, vale and mountain, flowery meadow,
 flashing sea,
Singing bird, and flowing fountain call us to rejoice in
 Thee.

Thou art giving and forgiving, ever blessing, ever
 blessed,
Wellspring of the joy of living, ocean depth of happy
 rest!

Thou our Father, Christ our Brother, all who live in
   love are Thine;
Teach us how to love each other; lift us to the joy
   divine.

Mortals, join the happy chorus, which the morning
   stars began;
Father-love is reigning o'er us, brother-love binds man
   to man.
Ever singing, march we onward, victors in the midst of
   strife;
Joyful music leads us sunward in the triumph song of
   life.

HENRY VAN DYKE

Dusk

IF YOU LOVE THE LAND, the place, more than love itself, the land has hold. Not the mind or heart, but the wildflowers, the diamonds on the lake, the trembling trees in storm, and the blue and gray and white sky that seems enclosed and expansive to all that is containable of heaven—these have hold.

Like turtles hanging akimbo in sun on decaying logs, waiting on sky's warmth to return to wet's deep, so I suppose our understanding comes: a soaking slow and rich and purposeful and sure, even in want, on cloudy days and in the hard desperation of winter.

In the light of a Southern summer sun, with its full saturation and languid magnificence, I am astonished and exalted at the power that such a land and place can have to bridle love. Yet I suspect that the land has even more wisdom, power, and authority than we attribute to her, and that she most certainly will bring us all, against our wild will, to consciousness again and again.

F. Lynne Bachleda

 *Dark*

I HAVE . . . A TERRIBLE NEED . . . shall I say the word?
. . . of religion. Then I go out at night and paint the stars.

Vincent van Gogh

Dawn

SAD SOUL, take comfort, nor forget
That sunrise never failed us yet.

CELIA THAXTER

Day

TO THE BREATH OF LIFE

Homage to you, Breath of Life, for the whole universe obeys you. You are the ruler of all things on earth, and the foundation of the earth itself.

Homage to you, Breath of Life, in the crashes of thunder and in the flashes of lightning. The rain you send gives food to the plants and drink to the animals.

Homage to you, Breath of Life, in the changing seasons, in the hot dry sunshine and the cold rain. There is comfort and beauty in every kind of weather.

The plants themselves rejoice in your bounty, praising you in the sweet smell of their blossom. The cattle rejoice, praising you in the pure white milk they give.

Homage to you, Breath of Life, in our breathing out and breathing in. At every moment, whatever we are doing, we owe you praise and thanksgiving.

Homage to you, Breath of Life, in our birth and in
our death. In the whole cycle of life you sustain and
inspire us.

Homage to you, Breath of Life, in the love and friend-
ship we enjoy. When we love one another, we reflect
your infinite love.

Men and women rejoice in your bounty, praising you
in poem and in song. The little children rejoice,
praising you in their innocent shrieks of laughter.

from Atharva Veda

Dusk

ALL YOU BIG THINGS, bless the Lord
Mount Kilimanjaro and Lake Victoria
The Rift Valley and the Serengeti Plain
Fat baobabs and shady mango trees
All eucalyptus and tamarind trees
Bless the Lord
Praise and extol Him for ever and ever.

All you tiny things, bless the Lord
Busy black ants and hopping fleas
Wriggling tadpoles and mosquito larvae
Flying locusts and water drops
Pollen dust and tsetse flies
Millet seeds and dried dagaa
Bless the Lord
Praise and extol Him for ever and ever.

Anonymous African chant

Dark

THE MOON'S the same old moon
The flowers exactly as they were
Yet I've become the thingness
Of all the things I see.

BUNAN, SEVENTEENTH-CENTURY JAPANESE BUDDHIST POET
from *The World of the Buddha*

 *Dawn*

WE NOW KNOW there are 100 billion stars in our galaxy and we have made contact with one billion other galaxies so far. What is clear from these facts alone is how vast our minds are, that they can make contact with such distances of space and time. Yet, as Itzhak Bentov points out, it may be that these billion-plus galaxies that we call our universe may be merely a "tiny cell in a much larger structure" and that even that much "vaster system is again just a speck in an even vaster system, and. . . ." We do not know the limits—but the fact that we can know there may be no imaginable limits itself suggests our own unlimits. In some way we are as space-less and time-less and as full of motion and energy that transforms itself in uncountable ways as is the universe itself. We can travel at speeds faster than light—though our senses cannot. Who dare say anymore where matter ends and energy begins? Or where matter ends and consciousness begins? Only those who have never traveled beyond the speed of light—in other words, those who have never loved or experienced insight.

MATTHEW FOX
from *A Spirituality Named Compassion:
Uniting Mystical Awareness with Social Justice*

THE MOST EXEMPLARY NATURE is that of the topsoil. It is very Christlike in its passivity and beneficence, and in the penetrating energy that issues out of its peaceableness. It increases by experience, by the passage of seasons over it, growth rising out of it and returning to it, not by ambition or aggressiveness. It is enriched by all things that die and enter into it. It keeps the past, not as history or as memory, but as richness, new possibility. Its fertility is always building up out of death into promise. Death is the bridge or the tunnel by which its past enters its future.

WENDELL BERRY
from *Recollected Essays 1965–1980*

THE INFINITY OF GOD

I see you in all things, O my God. Infinity itself is your
creation. And all around are the signs of your
infinity: the bursting life of countless plants; the
unending song of innumerable birds; the tireless
movement of animals and insects. Nowhere can I see
a beginning or an end of your creation.

I see the infinite beauty which infuses the entire
universe. You are the king of the universe, and its
beauty is your crown and scepter. I bow down in
homage and adoration.

You are immortal, imperishable, the summit of all
knowledge, the power behind all movement. You
designed all things, and set them in motion.

The sun is your eye during the day, and the moon your
eye at night. The wind is your breath, and the fertile
brown earth is your heart.

By your power all things are created, and by your power they are destroyed. Birth and death are in your hands. I tremble with awe and wonder when I contemplate your power.

As the waters of a river flow to the sea, the path determined by the line of the valley, so we pass through life to death, our destiny mapped out by your will.

Lord, reveal yourself to me. Show me that love, not hatred, inspires your creation. Show me that mercy, not anger, guides my life. I do not ask to understand the mystery of your works; I want only to be assured of your goodness.

from the Bhagavad Gita

Dark

LORD, THOU SENDEST DOWN RAIN upon the uncounted millions of the forest, and givest the trees to drink exceedingly. We are here upon this isle a few handfuls of men, and how many myriads upon myriads of stalwart trees! Teach us the lesson of the trees. The sea around us, which this rain recruits, teems with the race of fish; teach us, Lord, the meaning of the fishes. Let us see ourselves for what we are, one out of the countless number of the clans of thy handiwork. When we would despair, let us remember that these also please and serve Thee.

ROBERT LOUIS STEVENSON
from "Teach Us the Lesson of the Trees"
in *Prayers Written at Vailima*

SUNRISE: hidden by pines and cedars to the east: I saw the red flame of the kingly sun glaring through the black trees, not like dawn but like a forest fire. Then the sun became distinguished as a person and he shone silently and with solemn power through the branches, and the whole world was silent and calm.

THOMAS MERTON
from *Conjectures of a Guilty Bystander*

Day

NATURE'S INTENT is neither food, nor drink, nor clothing, nor comfort, nor anything else in which God is left
out. Whether you like it or not, whether you know it or
not, secretly nature seeks, hunts, tries to ferret out the
track on which God may be found.

MEISTER ECKHART

EARTH, isn't this what you want: to arise within us,
invisible? Isn't it your dream
to be wholly invisible someday?—O Earth: invisible!
What, if not transformation, is your urgent command?
Earth, my dearest, I will. Oh believe me, you no longer
need your springtimes to win me over—one of them,
ah even one, is already too much for my blood.
Unspeakably I have belonged to you, from the first.
You were always right, and your holiest inspiration
is our intimate companion, Death.
Look, I am living. On what? Neither childhood nor
    future
grows any smaller. . . . Superabundant being
wells up in my heart.

RAINER MARIA RILKE
from "The Ninth Duino Elegy"

 *Dark*

PROTECT ME, MY LORD; my boat is so small, and your ocean so big.

Breton fishermen's prayer

Dawn ☼

I HAVE A NEIGHBOR ON THE ISLAND WHO, to build his house, cleared his property with a bulldozer. Scraped it clean. Down to bare coral rock and sand. Not a blade of grass left standing. We humans have that much power. Nothing can bear our assault if we set our minds to destruction. But it is not just physical force that binds us to our fellow creatures. Our spirits, too, are linked. I do not mean to sound mystical. I am not talking about spirits as the disembodied souls of traditional religion, or as the vague cosmic resonances of New Age philosophy. I am talking about heart and mind as they are embedded in matter. When we cut our hearts and minds free from the web of life—from the green fuse—we sever our roots, and something fierce and flowing ceases to animate us. Our souls may be inextricably entangled with our bodies, but they are not bounded by the envelopes of our bodies. Our souls have roots in the ages, in the fusion of protons at the heart of the sun, in the burgeoning multiplicity of life. Our spirits throw out tendrils. We send runners. The growth of our spirit is—can be—lush, tropical. Our souls are bounded only by the limits of our knowledge.

CHET RAYMO
from *Natural Prayers*

Day

O HIDDEN LIFE, vibrant in every atom,
O Hidden Light, shining in every creature,
O Hidden Love, embracing all in Oneness,
May each who feels himself as one with Thee
Know he is therefore one with every other.

ANNIE BESANT, FOUNDER OF THE THEOSOPHICAL SOCIETY

SOLITUDE

There is a pleasure in the pathless woods,
There is a rapture on the lonely shore,
There is society where none intrudes,
By the deep Sea, and music in its roar.
I love not Man the less, but Nature more,
From these our interviews, in which I steal
From all I may be, or have been before,
To mingle with the Universe, and feel
What I can ne'er express, yet cannot all conceal.

LORD BYRON
from *Childe Harold's Pilgrimage*

 *Dark*

INTO THE WOODS my Master went,
Clean forspent, forspent.
Into the woods my Master came,
Forspent with love and shame.
But the olives they were not blind to him,
The little gray leaves were kind to him:
The thorn trees had a mind to him
When into the woods he came.

Out of the woods my Master went
And he was well content.
Out of the woods my Master came,
Content with death and shame,
When death and shame would woo him last,
From under the trees they drew him last:
'Twas on a tree they slew him—last
When out of the woods he came.

SIDNEY LANIER

BE A GARDENER

Be a gardener
Dig and ditch
Toil and sweat,
And turn the earth upside down
And seek the deepness
And water the plants in time.
Continue this work
And make sweet floods to run
And noble and abundant fruits
To spring.
Take this food and drink
And carry it to God
As your true worship.

JULIAN OF NORWICH

Day

LIGHT A HOLY FIRE

Receive this holy fire.
Make your lives like this fire.
A holy life that is seen.
A life of God that is seen.
A life that has no end.
A life that darkness does not overcome.
May this light of God in you grow.
Light a fire that is worthy of your heads.
Light a fire that is worthy of your children.
Light a fire that is worthy of your fathers.
Light a fire that is worthy of your mothers.
Light a fire that is worthy of God.
Now go in peace.
May the Almighty protect you today and all days.

ANONYMOUS MASAI PRAYER

Dusk ◠

WHENEVER I WALK WITH A CHILD, I think how much I have seen disappear in my own life. What will there be for this person when he is my age? If he senses something ineffable in the landscape, will I know enough to encourage it?—to somehow show him that, yes, when people talk about violent death, spiritual exhilaration, compassion, futility, final causes, they are drawing on forty thousand years of human meditation on this—as we embrace Douglas firs, or stand by a river across whose undulating back we skip stones, or dig out a camas bulb, biting down into a taste so much wilder than last night's potatoes.

The most moving look I ever saw from a child in the woods was on a mud bar by the footprints of a heron. We were on our knees, making handprints beside the footprints. You could feel the creek vibrating in the silt and sand. The sun beat down heavily on our hair. Our shoes were soaking wet. The look said: I did not know until now that I needed someone much older to confirm this, the feeling I have of life here. I can now grow older, knowing it need never be lost.

BARRY LOPEZ
from "Children in the Woods" in *Crossing Open Ground*

 *Dark*

BIRDFOOT'S GRAMPA

The old man
must have stopped our car
two dozen times to climb out
and gather into his hands
the small toads blinded
by our lights and leaping,
live drops of rain.

The rain was falling,
a mist about his white hair
and I kept saying
you can't save them all,
accept it, get back in
we've got places to go.

But, leathery hands full
of wet brown life,
knee deep in the summer
roadside grass,
he just smiled and said

they have places to go to
too.

JOSEPH BRUCHAC
from *Entering Onondaga*

 *Dawn*

CREATURES RISE, creatures vanish;
I alone am real, Arjuna,
looking out, amused, from deep
within the eyes of every creature.

from the Bhagavad Gita

DURING OPEN-DESERT CATTLE DRIVES, livestock sometimes suddenly turn and, with nostrils flared big as oranges, march in some random direction, undaunted by slaps and shouts from horseback riders. Hours or maybe a day later, far off course from the cattle drive, they reach water, pawing into its banks and inhaling it. Coyotes have been reported to trot over twenty miles straight to a water hole, deviating only to sleep or hunt rabbits. Omens and rumors are constant in the desert. It is all a matter of learning how to read them, and when to commit to walking straight across desolation to reach the right place.

CRAIG CHILDS
from *The Secret Knowledge of Water*

 *Dusk*

THE WIND

How lonesome the Wind must feel Nights—
When people have put out the Lights
And everything that has an Inn
Closes the shutter and goes in.

How pompous the Wind must feel Noons—
Stepping to incorporeal Tunes
Correcting errors of the sky
And clarifying scenery.

How mighty the Wind must feel Morns—
Encamping on a thousand dawns
Espousing each and spurning all
Then soaring to his Temple Tall.

EMILY DICKINSON

AND NOW MY WHOLE BEING breathes the wind, which blows through the belfry, and my hand is on the door through which I see the heavens. The door swings out upon a vast sea of darkness and of prayer. Will it come like this, the moment of my death? Will you open a door upon the great forest and set my feet upon a ladder under the moon, and take me out among the stars?

THOMAS MERTON
from *The Sign of Jonas*

 Dawn

EVER UPON THIS STAGE,
Is acted God's calm, annual drama.
Gorgeous processions, songs of birds,
Sunrise, that fullest feed and freshens most the soul,
The heaving sea, the waves upon the shore, the musical,
    strong waves,
The woods, the stalwart trees, the slender tapering trees,
The flowers, the grass, the lilliput, countless armies of
    the grass,
The heat, the showers, the measureless pasturages,
The scenery of the snows,
The wind's free orchestra,
The stretching, light-hung roof of clouds—the clear
    cerulean, and the bulging silver fringes,
The high dilating stars, the placid, beckoning stars,
The moving flocks and herds, the plains and emerald
    meadows,
The shows of all the varied lands, and all the growths
    and products.

. . . .

Loud O my throat, and clear, O soul!
The season of thanks.

WALT WHITMAN
from "A Carol of Harvest"

Day

THERE IS A CERTAIN FUTILITY in the efforts being made—truly sincere, dedicated, and intelligent efforts—to remedy our environmental devastation simply by activating renewable sources of energy and by reducing the deleterious impact of the industrial world. The difficulty is that the natural world is seen primarily for human use, not as a mode of sacred presence primarily to be communed with in wonder and beauty and intimacy. In our present attitude the natural world remains a commodity to be bought and sold, not a sacred reality to be venerated. The deep psychic change needed to withdraw us from the fascination of the industrial world, and the deceptive gifts that it gives us, is too difficult for simply the avoidance of its difficulties or the attractions of its benefits. Eventually only our sense of the sacred will save us.

THOMAS BERRY
from the introduction to *When the Trees Say Nothing: Writings on Nature by Thomas Merton*

Dusk

THE BIRDS HAVE VANISHED into the sky,
and now the last cloud drains away.

We sit together, the mountain and me,
until only the mountain remains.

LI-PO, EIGHTH-CENTURY TAOIST POET

 *Dark*

EVENING

(In words of one syllable)

The day is past, the sun is set,
And the white stars are in the sky;
While the long grass with dew is wet
And through the air the bats now fly.

The lambs have now lain down to sleep,
The birds have long since sought their nests;
The air is still; and dark, and deep
On the hill side the old wood rests.

Yet of the dark I have no fear,
But feel as safe as when 'tis light;
For I know God is with me there,
And He will guard me through the night.

For God is by me when I pray,
And when I close mine eyes in sleep,
I know that He will with me stay,
And will all night watch by me keep.

For he who rules the stars and sea,
Who makes the grass and trees to grow,
Will look on a poor child like me,
When on my knees I to Him bow.

He holds all things in His right hand,
The rich, the poor, the great, the small;
When we sleep, or sit, or stand,
Is with us, for He loves us all.

THOMAS MILLER

 *Dawn*

O GOD, we thank you for this earth, our home; for the wide sky and the blessed sun; for the salt sea and the running water; for the everlasting hills and the never resting winds; for trees and the common grass underfoot.

We thank you for our senses by which we hear the songs of birds, and see the splendor of the summer fields and taste of the autumn fruits and rejoice in the feel of the snow and smell the breath of the spring.

Grant us a heart wide open to all this beauty; and save our souls from being so blind that we pass unseeing when even the common thornbush is aflame with your glory, O God our creator, who lives and reigns forever and ever. Amen.

WALTER RAUSCHENBUSH

I DON'T THINK IT IS ENOUGH appreciated how much an outdoor book the Bible is. It is a "hypaethral book," such as Thoreau talked about—a book open to the sky. It is best read and understood outdoors, and the farther outdoors the better. Or that has been my experience of it. Passages that within walls seem improbable or incredible, outdoors seem merely natural. This is because outdoors we are confronted everywhere with wonders; we see that the miraculous is not extraordinary but the common mode of existence. It is our daily bread. Whoever really has considered the lilies of the field or the birds of the air and pondered the improbability of their existence in this warm world within the cold and empty stellar distances will hardly balk at the turning of water into wine—which was, after all, a very small miracle. We forget the greater and still continuing miracle by which water (with soil and sunlight) is turned into grapes.

WENDELL BERRY
from *Sex, Economy, Freedom & Community*

 *Dusk*

BUT LET MY SOUL PRAISE THEE that it may love
  Thee,
And let it tell Thee Thy mercies that it may praise Thee.
Without ceasing Thy whole creation speaks Thy praise—
The spirit of every man by the words that his mouth
  directs to Thee,
Animals and lifeless matter by the mouth of those who
  look upon them.
That so our soul rises out of its mortal weariness unto
  Thee,
Helped upward by the things Thou hast made
And passing beyond them unto Thee who has wonder-
  fully made them:
And there refreshment is and strength unfailing. Amen.

ST. AUGUSTINE

I LIVE IN THE WOODS out of necessity. I get out of bed in the middle of the night because it is imperative that I hear the silence of the night, alone, and, with my face on the floor, say psalms, alone, in the silence of the night . . . the silence of the forest is my bride and the sweet dark warmth of the whole world is my love and out of the heart of that dark warmth comes the secret that is heard only in silence, but it is the root of all the secrets that are whispered by all the lovers in their beds all over the world.

THOMAS MERTON
from *Dancing in the Water of Life: Seeking Peace in the Hermitage*

THE WASHING OF THE FEET

I thank you, dumb and silent stone,
I bend in reverence to you;
My life and growth as plant to you I owe,

I thank you, fruitful earth and flower,
I bow my head in reverence to you;
You helped me rise to animal's estate.

I thank you, stone and plant and beast,
I make obeisance lowly to you all;
'Tis you have helped me to my human self.

So flows thanksgiving ever back and forth
In the divine Whole, manifold yet One,
Entwining all with threads of thankfulness.

CHRISTIAN MORGENSTERN

TEN THOUSAND FLOWERS in spring, the moon in
   autumn,
a cool breeze in summer, snow in winter.
If your mind isn't clouded by unnecessary things,
this is the best season of your life.

WU-MEN, THIRTEENTH-CENTURY CHINESE ZEN MASTER

 *Dusk*

LORD, SINCE YOU HAVE TAKEN from me all earthly favors I can now see that you have left me with a spiritual gift beyond price, which every dog has by nature. You have made me faithful to you even at times of the greatest distress, bereft of all comforts. This faithfulness I cherish more fervently than all the riches of the world.

MECHTHILD OF MAGDEBURG
from "The Dog's Gift"

NIGHT

The sun descending in the west,
The evening star does shine,
The birds are silent in their nest,
And I must seek for mine.
    The moon, like a flower
    In heaven's high bower,
    With silent delight
    Sits and smiles on the night.

Farewell, green fields and happy grove,
Where flocks have ta'en delight;
Where lambs have nibbled, silent move
The feet of angels bright:
    Unseen, they pour blessing,
    And joy without ceasing,
    On each bud and blossom,
    On each sleeping bosom.

They look in every thoughtless nest
Where birds are covered warm;
They visit caves of every beast,

To keep them all from harm.
    If they see any weeping
    That should have been sleeping,
    They pour sleep on their head,
    And sit down by their bed.

When wolves and tigers howl for prey
They pitying stand and weep,
Seeking to drive their thirst away,
And keep them from the sheep.
    But if they rush dreadful,
    The angels, most heedful,
    Receive each mild spirit
    New worlds to inherit.

And there the lion's ruddy eyes
Shall flow with tears of gold:
And pitying the tender cries,
And walking round the fold,
    Saying: "Wrath by His meekness,
    And by His health, sickness,
    Are driven away
    From our immortal day.

"And now beside thee, bleating lamb,
I can lie down and sleep.
Or think on Him who bore thy name,
Graze after thee, and weep.
    For, washed in life's river,
    My bright mane for ever
    Shall shine like the gold,
    As I guard o'er the fold."

WILLIAM BLAKE

 *Dawn*

I HAD AN EXPERIENCE I CAN'T PROVE, I can't even explain it, but everything that I know as a human being, everything that I am tells me that it was real. I was part of something wonderful, something that changed me forever; a vision of the Universe that tells us undeniably how tiny, and insignificant, and how rare and precious we all are. A vision that tells us we belong to something that is greater than ourselves. That we are not, that none of us are, alone.

CARL SAGAN
from the screenplay for *Contact*;
the main character, Ellie Arroway, is speaking

Day

I **BELIEVE IN ONE GOD**—sole, eternal—He who, motionless, moves all the heavens with his love and his desire. . . .

This is the origin, this is the spark that then extends into a vivid flame and, like a star in heaven, glows in me.

DANTE ALIGHIERI
from canto XXIV, *Paradiso*

 *Dusk*

YOU ARE EVERYWHERE

God, you are everywhere
present invisible
near to us speaking—
the silence awaits you
mankind exists for you
men see and know you.

Men made of flesh and bone
men of light and of stone
men of hard stone and blood
a flow unstaunchable
mankind your people
our city on earth.

Earth is all that we are
dust is all that we make,
breathe into us, open us,
make us your earth
your heaven new made
your peace upon earth.

HUUB OOSTERHUIS

 *Dark*

REMEMBER

Remember the sky you were born under,
know each of the star's stories.
Remember the moon, know who she is.
Remember the sun's birth at dawn is the strongest point
    of time.
Remember sundown and the giving away to night.
Remember your birth, how your mother struggled
to give you form and breath. You are evidence of
her life, and her mother's, and hers.
Remember your father. He is your life also.
Remember the earth whose skin you are:
red earth, black earth, yellow earth, white earth
brown earth, we are earth.
Remember the plants, trees, animal life who all have
    their
tribes, their families, their histories, too. Talk to them,
listen to them. They are alive poems.
Remember the wind. Remember her voice. She knows
    the
origin of this universe. Remember you are all people
    and that all people are you.

Remember you are the universe and this universe is
    you.
Remember all is in motion, is growing, is you.
Remember language comes from this.
Remember the dance language is, that life is.
Remember.

JOY HARJO

THE SALUTATION OF THE DAWN

Listen to the Exhortation of the Dawn!
  Look to this Day!
For it is Life, the very Life of Life.
In its brief course lie all the
Verities and Realities of your Existence,
  The Bliss of Growth,
  The Glory of Action,
  The Splendor of Beauty,
For Yesterday is but a Dream,
And Tomorrow is only a Vision;
But Today well lived makes every
Yesterday a Dream of Happiness, and every
Tomorrow a Vision of Hope.
Look well therefore to this Day!
Such is the Salutation of the Dawn.

ANONYMOUS SANSKRIT TEXT

Day

MYSTICS THROUGHOUT TIME, in all traditions, have said the same thing. We do not have to search for God, because the presence of the Divine permeates all things. If there is a search at all, it is God searching for Itself.

RABBI DAVID COOPER
from *God Is a Verb: Kabbalah and the Practice of Mystical Judaism*

WHY DO I LIVE ALONE? I don't know. . . . In some mysterious way I am condemned to it. . . . I cannot have enough of the hours of silence when nothing happens. When the clouds go by. When the trees say nothing. When the birds sing. I am completely addicted to the realization that just being there is enough, and to add something else is to mess it all up. It would be so much more wonderful to be all tied up in someone . . . and I know inexorably that this is not for me. It is a kind of life from which I am absolutely excluded. I can't desire it. I can only desire this absurd business of trees that say nothing, of birds that sing, of a field in which nothing ever happens (except perhaps that a fox comes and plays, or a deer passes by). This is crazy. It is lamentable. I am flawed, I am nuts. I can't help it. Here I am, now, . . . happy as a coot. The whole business of saying I am flawed is a lie. I am happy. I cannot explain it. . . . Freedom, darling. This is what the woods mean to me. I am free, free, a wild being, and that is all that I ever can really be. I am dedicated to it, addicted to it, sworn to it, and sold to it. It is the freedom in me that loves you.

THOMAS MERTON
from *Learning to Love: Exploring Solitude and Freedom*

 *Dark*

SOME THINGS I DO KNOW with unbridled certainty. It is the sunshine that gives me hope for the possibility of a peaceful world. It is the breeze that whispers the sacred to me. It is the ground that gives me all the present and future I can grasp. It is the water that permits holiness to permeate into my marrow, cleansing me for new beginnings day after day. No cathedral is closer or more magnificent than the earth. How can I be anything but grateful for the ways I need the nature of this world?

F. Lynne Bachleda

Rights and Permissions

The editor and publisher gratefully acknowledge the following sources for permission to use copyrighted material and for their cooperation in fair use and public domain applications. Extensive effort has been made to trace copyright holders, and the publisher would be grateful to hear from any copyright holders not acknowledged.

Bibliography

These fine anthologies were an invaluable source of inspiration and material. I am grateful to the editors and publishers.

Allen, Paul M., and Joan deRis, eds., *Francis of Assisi's Canticle of the Creatures: A Modern Spiritual Path.* New York: Continuum, 1996.

Appleton, George, ed., *The Oxford Book of Prayer.* New York: Oxford University Press, 1985.

Batchelor, Mary, ed., *The Doubleday Prayer Collection.* New York: Doubleday, 1996.

Brussat, Frederic, and Mary Ann Brussat, eds., *Spiritual Literacy: Reading the Sacred in Everyday Life.* New York: Simon & Schuster, 1996.

Ford-Grabowsky, Mary, ed., *Sacred Voices: Essential Women's Wisdom Through the Ages.* New York: HarperSanFrancisco, A Division of HarperCollins Publishers, 2002.

Freke, Timothy, ed., *The Illustrated Book of Sacred Scriptures.* Wheaton, IL: Godsfield Press/Quest Books, 1998.

Harvey, Andrew, ed., *Teachings of the Christian Mystics.* Boston: Shambhala, 1998.

Hogan, Julie K., ed., *The Ideals Treasury of Prayer.* Nashville: Ideals Publications Inc., 2000.

Law, Philip, ed., *Saviour: The Life of Christ in Words and Paintings.* Chicago: Loyola Press, 2000.

Mitchell, Stephen, ed., *The Enlightened Heart: An Anthology of Sacred Poetry.* New York: HarperPerennial, A Division of HarperCollins Publishers, 1989.

Philip, Neil, ed., *The New Oxford Book of Children's Verse.* New York: Oxford University Press, 1996.

Reagan, Michael, ed., *The Hand of God: Thoughts and Images Reflecting the Spirit of the Universe.* Atlanta: Lionheart Books, 1999.

Tutu, Desmond, ed., *An African Prayer Book.* New York: Doubleday, 1995.

Van de Weyer, Robert, ed., *The HarperCollins Book of Prayers: A Treasury of Prayers Through the Ages.* New York: HarperSanFrancisco, A Division of HarperCollins Publishers, 1993.

Index of Authors and Sources

Index of Titles and First Lines